AFFILIATE MARKETING FOR BEGINNERS

A step-by-step process of making money online even from the comfort of your home.

Ryan Hale

Copyright

All rights reserved. No part of this publication may be reproduced, stored or transmitted in any form or by any means, electronic, mechanical, photocopying, recording, scanning, or otherwise without written permission from the publisher. It is illegal to copy this book, post it to a website, or distribute it by any other means without permission.

Copyright © Ryan Hale 2024

TABLE OF CONTENT

Introduction

Chapter One: Introduction To Affiliate Marketing

Chapter Two: Getting traffic:

– Paid Traffic

– Organic traffic

Chapter Three: Mentality Boost

Chapter Four: Advertising

Chapter Five: Funneling

Chapter Six: Audience Building/Lead Generation

INTRODUCTION

Making money online is possible with your smartphone or whatever you have as a device, you can actually make dollars every day.

In the online world, there is so much to learn and work if you're looking for strategies and techniques to make money daily as an affiliate marketer.

This book is a perfect plug for you, inside you find a step-by-step process on how to choose the right products to promote, how to create effective marketing campaigns and how to build a loyal audience of potential buyers.

Whether you are new to affiliate marketing or looking to take your earnings to the next level, This book is a success tip for anyone in the online space (Affiliate marketing to be precise.)

CHAPTER ONE

INTRODUCTION TO AFFILIATE MARKETING

Affiliate marketing is a performance-based marketing strategy that involves promoting other people's or company's products or services and earning a commission for every successful sale made through your unique link.

As an affiliate marketer, you partner with a company or individual that has a product or service to sell, and you promote it through various channels such as social media, email marketing, blog posts, or paid advertising.

When someone clicks on your affiliate link and makes a purchase of the product, you earn a percentage of the sale as a commission.

Affiliate marketing is a popular way for business owners to increase their sales and for individuals to earn massive income online and there are various strategies you can use as much as earning $100 weekly for a start.

CHAPTER TWO

TRAFFIC IN AFFILIATE MARKETING

Traffic in marketing refers to the number of visitors or users that visit a website, social media platform or other digital platforms. This includes organic and paid traffic.

Traffic is an important metric as an affiliate, as it includes the reach and popularity of a website or platform. Affiliate marketers can use various tactics to increase traffic such as SEO (search engine optimization), content marketing, social media marketing, email marketing, Video marketing (making/editing videos of your products) and paid advertising.

Ultimately, the goal is to drive more traffic to a platform to increase brand awareness, generate leads and drive sales.

We have two types of traffic,

paid and organic traffic.

1. Paid traffic: paid traffic can be a great way to boost your affiliate marketing efforts as it helps you reach a larger audience than relying solely on organization traffic.

Here are a few tips for effective use of paid traffic in your affiliate marketing strategy.

Choose the right platform: There are many platforms you can use for paid traffic, including social media Ads, Google Ads and native Ads. Consider your target audience and where they are more likely to be spending their time online.

Set a budget: Determine how much you can afford to spend on paid traffic and set a budget accordingly, keep in mind that it may take some trial and error to find the most effective approach.

Select the right offer: Choose an affiliate product that is a good fit for your niche/target audience, and it's likely to convert well with paid traffic.

Create compelling Ads copy: Make sure your ads copy is eye-catching and highlights the benefit of the product or service you are promoting.

Optimize your landing page: Your landing page should be optimized for conversion and make it easy for users to take your desired actions.

Remember, paid traffic can be a powerful tool when used correctly, but it's important to approach it strategically and with a clear plan in place.

2. Organic traffic: it's a highly valuable source that compels visitors to your page or offer because it involves attracting users who are genuinely interested in the content or products you are promoting through natural search engine results. I have some guaranteed keys to increase your organic traffic to your page/site.

Consistent content creation: Regularly creating high quality, engaging, informative content around your niche helps drive traffic to your site. This content can also help establish trust among your readers.

Keyword research: Researching relevant and high traffic keywords related to your niche and products, adding them to your content can help you rank higher on search engines results pages.

Optimize your website for SEO: This involves updating website structure, Facebook tags and ensuring your website is mobile-friendly.

This helps your chances of ranking better on search engines.

Share your content on social media: Sharing your content on all social media platforms can help drive traffic to your website from your followers and increase your exposure to a broader audience.

Build back-links: build back-links to your websites by guest blogging, participating in relevant forums, groups and so on.

Also, collaborating with other bloggers to help you establish domain authority and increase your visibility.

It is significant to record all traffic connections, you get to know which tactics work better for you as an affiliate.

CHAPTER THREE

MENTALITY BOOST

Now before going into any business you must have the right mentality and also know the pain point of your audience.

As a marketer, it's essential to stay motivated and maintain a positive mindset to achieve success.

Set clear and achievable goals: Goal setting is crucial in keeping you motivated and focused. Ensure onset realistic and achievable goals to avoid discouragement and frustration.

Celebrate your achievements: Always acknowledge your successes and celebrate them, no matter how small they may seem. This helps keep you in a position and reinforce the idea that you are capable of reaching your goal.

Surround yourself with positivity: Surround yourself with people who inspire and encourage you, for instance, I have an amazing parent that wouldn't want me to go astray. They always encourage and advise me positively in achieving my goals.

For me to be able to write a book is because I have positive people around me, having positive people around you boosts you to achieve what's already in you.

Avoid negativity as much as possible. This includes negative news, social media drama and other sources of negativity that may affect your ability to stay focused and motivated.

Focus on your personal development: Invest in yourself, learn new skills and stay up to date with the latest trends in your industry (affiliate marketing world) to help boost your confidence and motivation.

Take breaks: Take short breaks throughout the day and longer breaks when needed so as not to shut down in the quest for a livelihood. Taking breaks helps alleviate burnouts and keeps you energized and focused.

Self-care: Take care of your physical and emotional well-being, be stable in your body, soul and spirit to think straight. You can also do that through exercise, eating healthy and getting enough sleep.Remember you need to stay fit first before making money. This helps you stay alert and focused during work hours.

Experiments: selling is 80% mindset and 20% strategy, value is exchange for money. Don't be afraid to take risks that will positively influence your business

Always try new methods and ways to improve your sales and promotion, don't remain bent on using one strategy you know, meanwhile there are a lot of fast selling strategies out there you could use to make sales massively, think big and broadly as an affiliate marketer.

Learn from your mistakes: There is no genuine rich man today that doesn't have a sad story to tell before his riches started flowing. They also went through hard times but persisted until they got to the height they are now.

Success does not come easy, it takes hard work and diligence to be successful, learn from the mistakes you make and re-strategies, don't get bogged down in the details, keep your goal in mind, which is to make sales as an affiliate and work towards a step at a time. "Rome was not built in a day.", " A journey of a thousand miles begins with a step."

CHAPTER FOUR

ADVERTISING

Advertising in affiliate marketing involves promoting merchant's products or services through various marketing channels such as social media, email marketing, paid advertising, which is also known as traffic generation and content marketing.

Affiliates earn a commission for every sale they generate for the merchant. To start advertising in affiliate marketing, you need to join an affiliate program that best suits your audience or niche (just like myself, I sell digital products.) it can be any kind of product.

Look for companies that offer high commission rates, quality products or services and reliable tracking and reporting tools

Once you have joined an affiliate company, you can start promoting the merchant's products or services through your chosen marketing channels. It's important to create high-quality content that resonates with your audience and include affiliate links to track your referrals.

To maximize your earnings in affiliate marketing, you should continuously optimize your marketing strategies, test different channels and campaigns and monitor your performance metrics.

You can also leverage affiliate networks, platforms, and pages/groups that provide additional resources and support for affiliates.

CHAPTER FIVE

FUNNELLING

Funneling is the ability to bring an audience together and sieve out the unimportant ones.

It's also a process of guiding potential customers through step by step or actions that ultimately lead to a sale.

The goal of a funnel is to create a clear path for potential customers to follow, with each step designed to move them closer to making a purchase from you. The first step in creating a funnel is identifying your target audience and understanding their needs and interests.

Also know their "PAS"=Pain, Agitate, Solve their problems.

This will help you to create relevant content and offer that is appealing. Next, you create a landing page or website that is designed to capture the attention of a potential customer and encourage them to act. This could be a page that offers a free download, a direct discount code or a special offer.

Once you have captured your audience's attention, you can now guide them through a series of steps that will help them to learn more about your product or services you are promoting and ultimately make a purchase.

This could include providing them with additional information about the benefit of your products, offering customer testimonials about the benefit of your product, offering customer reviews and testimonials, providing clear calls that will remove doubts from them and encourage them to take actions.

Overall, the key to success in affiliate marketing is to create a funnel that is tailored to the needs and interests of your target audience, and that provides them with a clear and compelling path to making a purchase.

CHAPTER SIX

LEAD GENERATION/ AUDIENCE BUILDING

Lead generation is an essential aspect of affiliate marketing.it involves identifying potential customers for the product or services you're promoting and getting them to act such as specifically filling out a form and making a purchase.

You need to know these strategies that will help in lead generation.

1. Develop lead magnets: offering a lead magnet, such as an e-book or a free trial,it's an effective way to attract potential customers and collect their contact information for further persuasion.

2. Create a landing page: Set up your social media accounts in a way that is eye - catching,stop posting randomly on your wall.

A dedicated landing page for your affiliate products and promotions can increase your conversion rates,make sure your landing page is optimized for lead generation by including a clear call-to-action(CTA) and a lead capture format.

3. Run paid advertising: paid advertising can be an effective way to generate leads quickly.Platforms like Google Ads, Facebook Ads and Instagram Ads allow you to target a specific audience and track your results.

4. Leverage influencer marketing: Partnering with influencers in your niche can help you reach a wider audience and generate more leads.

Don't forget influencer marketing is also a part of paid traffic, make sure the influencer you work with aligns with your brand and has an engaged follower.

5. Use Email marketing: Email marketing is an effective way to nurture your leads and turn them into customers, create a lead magnet and use it to build your email list. Then send targeted emails to subscribers(Leads) to encourage them to make a purchase.

N/B: All these processes are vital in making your first $100 weekly as an affiliate marketer or even as a newbie in the system, remember your hardwork will pay off, if you are diligent enough to use all the processes written In this book.

Leverage on the online world and see yourself grow financially

Thank You For Reading

www.ingramcontent.com/pod-product-compliance
Lightning Source LLC
Chambersburg PA
CBHW071001220526
45471CB00007B/3132